# BASKETBALL HALL OF FAMERS

## BILL BRADLEY

### James Buckley Jr.

the rosen publishing group's
rosen
central

*This book is dedicated to student athletes who*
*properly balance schoolwork and sports.*

Published in 2002 by The Rosen Publishing Group, Inc.
29 East 21st Street, New York, NY 10010

First Edition

**Library of Congress Cataloging-in-Publication Data**

Buckley, James, Jr.
Bill Bradley / by James Buckley, Jr.
p. cm. — (Basketball Hall of Famers)
Includes bibliographical references and index.
Summary: Profiles the life of William Bradley, a Princeton
University Rhodes Scholar and NBA All-Star who was a successful
basketball player for the New York Knicks before becoming a
United States Senator.
ISBN 0-8239-3479-9 (lib. bdg.)
1. Bradley, Bill, 1943– —Juvenile literature. 2. Basketball players—
United States—Biography—Juvenile literature. 3. New York
Knickerbockers (Basketball team)—History—Juvenile literature. [1.
Bradley, Bill, 1943– 2. Legislators. 3. Basketball players.]
I. Title. II. Series.
GV884.B7 B83 2001
796.323'092—dc21

2001003211

*Manufactured in the United States of America*

# contents

# Introduction

Few Americans have enjoyed success as gracefully as Bill Bradley. As a basketball player, he reached the top of his sport in both the amateur and professional ranks. As a politician, he was a respected three-term United States senator. As a writer, he has written several well-regarded books. To succeed in any one of these fields would have been enough for most people, but not for William Warren Bradley.

Bradley's life reads like a novel. Bradley first came to the attention of the basketball world at Princeton University in the early 1960s. He later led the United States to a gold medal in the sport at the 1964 Summer

Bill Bradley, shown here playing for Princeton in 1964, is an accomplished basketball player, scholar, and legislator.

Olympics. After studying and playing basketball in England and Europe for two years, he joined the National Basketball Association (NBA), where he secured two league championships for the New York Knicks. Later, Bradley left the NBA, ran for public office representing New Jersey, and eventually served the state as a senator for eighteen years. When his time in the Senate was completed, he wrote and taught for several years before reentering politics in 2000 when he ran for the U.S. presidency. He eventually conceded the Democratic nomination to Vice President Al Gore. It was one of the few times in Bradley's life that he did not succeed.

It's hard to believe that all of these events could have happened to one person. How does one go from a tiny town in Missouri to membership in the Basketball Hall of Fame to a seat on the floor of the U.S. Senate, not to mention success as a gifted writer and teacher?

In Bradley's case, it was by combining three key elements: a sharp and thoughtful mind, a sense of responsibility and curiosity about the world, and a real caring for people. Of course, being six feet five inches tall and having a sweet outside shot helps make the game of basketball a little simpler.

Those three qualities—intelligence, responsibility, and caring—have been the center of Bradley's entire life: in basketball and in politics, in his private life, and in his writing. The roots of these traits can be traced to Bradley's childhood. As he grew up, those parts of his personality were sharpened, defined, and built by the events of his life. At every step of his journey, he learned and grew, whether it was at college, while traveling the world, while playing in the NBA, or while serving in the U.S. Senate.

At every step, Bradley used his talents—and an incredible capacity for hard work—to succeed. But it wasn't medals, or trophies, or prestige that drove Bradley to succeed; it was his own personal integrity. He believed that no matter what the outcome, he would always be a success.

# The Kid from Crystal City

Bill Bradley's remarkable story begins in the heartland of America. He was born on July 28, 1943, in Crystal City, Missouri, about thirty-five miles south of St. Louis. Crystal City was a small, working-class town of about 3,500 people with a huge glass factory as its centerpiece. His father, Warren, was the president of the local bank, having worked his way up from teller during many years of service. His mother, Susie, was a fourth-grade teacher and volunteered for many organizations in town, including serving as a Sunday-school teacher.

In his book *Time Present, Time Past*, Bradley recalls how, many years after his mother retired from teaching, people would still

Bill Bradley receives a hometown hero's welcome at Crystal City High School in Missouri during his bid for the presidency in 1999.

visit to tell her how much her skills had shaped their lives.

Warren Bradley's story illustrates where Bill learned his dedication to hard work. Warren was forced to quit school at sixteen to help support his family. He worked at the local railroad before joining the bank at the age of twenty. Though not as educated as other bank workers, Warren constantly looked for ways to improve himself. Over many years, he advanced, earning higher positions. Finally, after sixteen years, he was named president of the bank and soon became its largest stockholder.

In *Time Present, Time Past,* Bradley recalls many stories of how his father helped local people by loaning them money, and how he learned about trust and responsibility from watching his father.

## An Early Love of Athletics

Bill was Warren and Susie's only son. From early on, they taught him that study and success in school were more important than any other activities. Bill Bradley's natural intelligence and dedication helped make him a straight-A student. He enjoyed many sports, but basketball soon became his favorite.

Part of his interest in the game came from his mother. Susie Bradley had been a top basketball player in high school and bought Bill his first basket. She helped a local man put it up on the side of their house and then helped put it to good use.

"Twenty years after her high school triumphs, my mother still considered herself a player," Bradley writes in his book *Values of the Game*. "She still wanted to win when we played one on one. Once when I was in the seventh grade, she gave me a little push going for a steal, and I pushed her back—to my horror, she slipped and banged her head on the asphalt. I was petrified, but she just got up and smiled."

Susie Bradley wasn't the only tough one in young Bill's house. Warren suffered throughout his life from painful arthritis. He could work, but he had trouble sleeping. Many everyday

During childhood, Bill Bradley (number 25) had a passion for basketball instilled in him by his mother, who had been a top player in high school.

activities, like tying his shoes or getting dressed, were very difficult for him. Bill and Susie had to help Warren do many things. Warren even had to use a pair of long wooden tweezers to pick up objects from the floor because he couldn't bend. Bill learned how to work through difficulty by watching his courageous father deal with his health problems.

Susie also made sure that Bill learned other skills, such as how to play the French horn and the piano. He also took classes in swimming, boxing, and French.

"My father, however, said no to dancing lessons," Bradley writes in *Time Present, Time Past*. "But my mother says to this day that I would have had better coordination as a basketball player if I'd taken ballet."

Young Bill's interest in sports continued to grow. He played baseball, his father's favorite game. When he was nine, he played basketball for the first time at the Crystal City YMCA. As he grew taller, basketball became his primary game. By the time he was a junior in high school, he had reached his full height of six feet five inches.

He loved listening to the radio, especially the reports of Edward R. Murrow, who made a series of programs re-creating famous historical events. Bill also spent hours reading his parents' old *Life*, *Look*, and *National Geographic* magazines. He began to imagine a world far away from Crystal City. Little did he know that it would be his basketball skills that would first help him see that world.

# Life Lessons

When Bill was fourteen years old, he went to a summer basketball camp in St. Louis, Missouri. The camp was organized by a former pro player named "Easy" Ed McCauley. At that camp, among players bigger, stronger, and older than he was, Bill held his own. And he learned that success in basketball came not just from size or strength, but from practice.

"If you're not practicing," McCauley told the campers, "remember—someone, somewhere is practicing. And when you two meet, if you have equal ability, he will win."

That was a turning point for Bill Bradley. From then on, intense practice became normal for him. In his books, he details the lengthy series of practices he created for himself, apart from anything else he was doing with his team. He became known for showing this level of dedication, a sense of personal ethics that would help him create a few unusual habits.

"I would wear glasses that prevented me from seeing the ball, and I would put chairs in

Bradley takes to the air in hopes of scoring a point for Crystal City High School in his Missouri hometown.

the gym and dribble around the chairs with the glasses on," he said in an NBA.com interview. "When I was walking down the street, I kept my eyes facing forward to learn to use my peripheral vision to see what was in the store windows."

He also did jumping drills with weights on his shoes. He stacked up chairs and pretended they were seven-foot-tall players to shoot over. He always attempted and made twenty-five baskets in a row. "If I missed the twenty-third," he writes, "I'd start all over from one."

It was hard work. It took time away from his friends and family, but not from his schoolwork. Though his mother and father spent every summer in Palm Beach, Florida—partly for Warren's health—Bill stayed behind to practice basketball.

"The by-product of those countless hours of practice was a self-discipline that carried over into every aspect of my life," he writes in *Time Present, Time Past*.

It also paid off on the court. Bill led his Crystal City High School team to their greatest triumphs. In those days, the Missouri high school state tournament invited all the schools together, large and small. Most often, teams from larger high schools won, since they had more players to choose from.

But in Bill's senior year, Crystal City made the state championship finals, defeating several teams but losing to one from St. Louis.

Life in little Crystal City was coming to a close for Bill Bradley. His basketball skills meant that colleges were offering him athletic scholarships. More than seventy-five schools offered to pay his tuition, room, and board. Bill knew that he could go anywhere he wanted, but his decision was based on more than basketball.

"When I was in high school, I certainly wanted to win the state championship," he said on NBA.com. "But I didn't think about playing professionally, even when I was practicing three hours a day." In other words, basketball for Bill was a way for him to challenge himself. He wasn't going to let it define who he was.

As he looked at the many offers, he also looked for schools with great academic reputations. Finally, not long before he graduated from high school, Bradley accepted a scholarship from Duke University in Durham, North Carolina.

But before he went to Duke, however, he went on a trip that would change his life.

# Bon Voyage!

Warren Bradley thought that a European vacation would be a good graduation present for his son. As a result, that June, Bill Bradley sailed on the *Queen Elizabeth* ocean liner to England. (Not one to miss an opportunity to practice, he spent many hours on the Atlantic crossing dribbling up and down the ship's long, narrow corridors.) He was awestruck by what he saw.

The places he had heard about on the radio and read about in books and magazines were as real as Crystal City. He went to England, to Italy, and to Germany. Most important, he went to Oxford, England.

Bill Bradley arrives in Southampton, England, on his way to Oxford University to be a Rhodes scholar.

Oxford is home to Oxford University, one of the most respected places for higher learning in the world. Bill knew, just by its atmosphere, that that was where he wanted to return and study someday.

After he got back to Crystal City from Europe, he broke his foot while practicing, and that injury sealed his decision. As his foot mended, and he couldn't play basketball for a while, he saw what life might be like without the game. He wondered, "If not for basketball, where would I most like to go to college?" The answer was Princeton University. Part of the reason was that Princeton turned out more Rhodes scholars than any other school. Rhodes scholars are chosen through many tough tests to attend Oxford University after college. Bill wanted to be one of them.

And so the kid from Crystal City who never stopped practicing, the kid who couldn't wait to see what the world had to offer him, left that summer for the next great adventure of his life.

# A Tiger's Tale

When Bradley began his college career, one story shows how much he valued his education over basketball: He arrived on campus at Princeton without visiting the basketball coach. As far as Princeton coach Butch van Breda Kolff knew, Bradley had chosen Duke. The young Missouri star, who was called good enough to play in the pros right out of high school by an official with the NBA's St. Louis Hawks, passed van Breda Kolff on campus and told him he'd be coming out for the team.

The coach was stunned. Princeton, being an Ivy League school, could not offer Bradley any scholarship money. Warren Bradley would pay for all of his son's education. But the younger Bradley had chosen to attend Princeton and play for the Tigers because of other reasons. Of course, van Breda Kolff was elated, too, and soon, so was the entire Princeton community, and the rest of the college basketball world.

One of the most successful and amazing college hoops careers ever began very quietly, as Bradley played for the Princeton freshman team. In those days, freshmen at most schools couldn't play for the varsity teams. And in Bradley's case, it's probably a good thing he wasn't thrown in with the older players right away. For the first time in his life, he struggled academically.

## Hitting the Books and the Basket

Although he had had a good education at Crystal City High School, many of his classmates at Princeton had attended high-level prep schools in the East. They were further ahead of him in many subjects, and he had to work very hard to catch up. Of course, hard work was nothing new to Bradley. He hunkered down in the library, stopped playing a second sport—freshman baseball—and made it through. In *Values of the Game*, he credits the work habits he picked up on the basketball court for having helped him succeed in his studies at Princeton.

As an athlete, he was already turning heads in many ways. Freshman basketball was normally not a very big deal. Few people watched, and the games didn't count for much. But with the attraction of Bradley's superior skills at shooting, passing, and dribbling, fans began flocking to the games. Bradley's teammates were impressed, too. He had tremendous passing ability and was able to give his teammates the ball sometimes before they knew they were open.

He consistently scored points in the games, even though he saw one of his main jobs as passing to teammates. Bradley was such a student of the game, and he had practiced so many skills for so long, that simply firing up

shots wasn't in him. Only when his team trailed at the end of a game did he take over and shoot whenever possible. This unselfish play made him a favorite with teammates, but it often drove victory-hungry coaches and fans crazy.

As a freshman, Bradley also set a record for basketball at every level—varsity or pro— by making fifty-seven consecutive free throws. He would remain an outstanding free-throw shooter throughout his career.

By his junior season, Bradley was one of the top college players in the country. He led the nation in scoring as a junior and helped Princeton University win the Ivy League title and earn a place in the postseason national playoffs. He continued to work diligently in school, too, gaining high marks in his classes, many of which focused on history, politics, and government, now his favorite subjects.

In addition, he began teaching Sunday school to teenagers, no matter how much midnight studying he had to do the previous night. Bradley's faith in God was another

Bill Bradley strolls on the Oxford University campus while studying law at the prestigious school.

driving force for him, but a private one. Yet without that inner strength, he often wrote in later years, he didn't think he could have accomplished all that he did.

His basketball skills, amazingly, improved from their already high level. His defense was one weak point coming out of high school, but by his senior year at Princeton, he was a top defender. His rebounding skills also improved.

One story, as told by writer John McPhee, shows just how carefully Bradley treated his practice and his sport. In McPhee's book, *A Sense of Where You Are*, he writes that Bradley had to practice during the summer of 1964 at a local high school while Princeton's gym was being repaired. He shot and shot, but his shots didn't seem to be falling right. He finally left, telling McPhee that the basket must be too short; he couldn't be missing that badly.

McPhee went back later with a ladder and a tape measure. The basket was one and one-eighth inches too low. Bradley had been right.

While interviewing Bradley, McPhee took him to an eye specialist who discovered that the basketball star had stunning peripheral vision, a measure of what can be seen at the edges of one's field of vision. The exercises that Bradley had done as a child—walking down the street looking straight ahead, while trying to look in windows at the same time—may have paid off. The doctor found that Bradley's peripheral vision was 15 degrees more than normal to the side and nearly 30 degrees more upward. This might explain why Bradley could see passing opportunities that his teammates couldn't.

At Princeton, Bradley was universally loved and respected as an athlete, as a student, and as a person. In an article in the *Princeton Alumni Weekly (PAW)* in 1965, two of his fellow students, B. Franklin Burgess and James Markham, wrote about how every student on campus wanted Bradley to know his or her name. The writers described how Bradley was the only person asked to join each of the sixteen "eating clubs" at Princeton during a process

A Tiger's Tale

called Bicker. These clubs were mostly social organizations that students were sometimes asked to join before their junior year. Normally, only a few clubs asked each student, but everyone wanted Bradley.

## A Growing Esteem for Politics

After leading Princeton to a second Ivy League title as a junior and leading the nation in scoring with a 32.3 points-per-game average, Bradley worked in Washington, D.C., over the summer. While helping out at the offices of Pennsylvania governor William Scranton and Congressman Richard Schweiker of Pennsylvania, he learned more about national politics. He spent memorable afternoons on the floor of the U.S. Senate, listening to debates and discussions. Even then, he was considering what his life would be like after Princeton, and a career in politics was a strong possibility. He also worked very hard on his senior thesis, a long, well-researched article that conveys a specific point of view.

29

Bradley prepares to make a basket for Princeton in 1965.

The topic of his paper was the U.S. Senate campaign of Harry S. Truman in 1940. In the *PAW* article, Bradley's adviser on his thesis, Professor Arthur Link, said about his famous student, "He has organization, self-discipline, intensity, drive, ambition to excel, and tremendous enthusiasm."

Those same qualities also drove him to continue to practice basketball during the summer. His talents earned him a spot on the U.S. Olympic team that would travel to Tokyo for the 1964 Summer Games. The team was made up of eleven players who had graduated and Bradley, the only player still in college. The team dominated their competition, though it was left to Bradley to seal a victory against Yugoslavia with three baskets late in the semi-final game.

In the gold-medal final, Bradley held the best player from the opposing Soviet Union team to only 8 points, and the United States won with a score of 73–59. The win sustained the United States's unbroken record of

Players from the University of Pennsylvania were no match for Bradley—shown here going for a basket—during the Ivy League championships in March 1964.

victories in Olympic basketball, a streak that would not end until 1972.

True to form, Bradley took the trip to Tokyo as an opportunity to learn. First, he spoke at length with several Soviet players by asking an Australian player to interpret. He was interested to hear about life in the Soviet Union and about the state of that nation.

Second, through a program called Princeton in Asia, he went on a tour of Taiwan and Hong Kong, among other places, after the Games, speaking at schools and universities about his Christian life and about America.

But even with all those accomplishments, his greatest moments on a college basketball court were still to come. After two seasons as an all-American and with an Olympic gold medal around his neck, Bradley was now a national hero. *Sports Illustrated* did a big feature on him before a Christmas tournament in New York City. Writer Frank Deford, a 1961 Princeton alumnus, wrote, "Bradley is almost too good to be true."

## A Future Foretold

At that Christmas tournament, Bradley's Princeton Tigers faced the Michigan Wolverines, led by another all-American player, Cazzie Russell. The game was a peek into the future in several ways. It was Bradley's first game at Madison Square Garden, where he would play for many years with the New York Knicks and where Russell would be his teammate. Michigan also would be Princeton's opponent in a big game near the end of the season.

Bradley dazzled fans at the Christmas tournament. He seemed unstoppable, scoring 41 points before fouling out with Princeton ahead and less than five minutes of game time remaining. Without Bradley, Princeton surrendered the lead, losing to Michigan by 2 points.

In the 1964–1965 Ivy League season, Princeton was cruising toward their third straight title. Bradley was racking up huge point totals— 41 against Dartmouth, 36 against both University of Pennsylvania and Columbia—but he also suffered his first injury, a seriously bruised thigh and knee, in January. Though he played through the pain, he was not the same. Oddly, the injury helped the Princeton Tigers improve. They learned that they could succeed without solely depending on Bradley.

At his last home game at Princeton's tiny gym, thousands of fans cheered. The Tigers defeated the University of Pennsylvania, and Bradley was carried on his teammates' shoulders to cut down the net, showing that they had won the Ivy League title once again.

John McPhee wrote the story of how Princeton students presented Bradley with a special trophy: the clapper, or pendulum, from a 200-year-old bell at Nassau Hall on Princeton's campus. They wanted him to always have a part of Princeton, and for Princeton to always be a part of him.

Bradley had broken every collegiate record. He was named to the all-American team for the third time (only the third player at the time so honored) and was named national player of the year. Yet, amazingly, he had one more stunning run of college play ahead of him.

By winning the Ivy League, Princeton advanced to the National Collegiate Athletic Association (NCAA) Tournament. Ivy League teams normally won one or two games in this tournament among the nation's top college basketball teams. In the first round, Princeton and Bradley played poorly, but

During a game against Wichita State in March 1965, Princeton player William Kock *(left)* passes to Bradley, who went on to score a two-pointer.

defeated Penn State by a score of 60–58. They then surprised a much stronger North Carolina State team by a score of 68–48.

"While we were watching Bradley," McPhee quotes N.C. State coach Press Maravich as saying, "he'd hit the open man behind us. It was as if he had us hypnotized."

Their next game was against the top-ranked Providence University team. No one really expected Princeton to win, even though they had had a great season. Still, all of the lessons the team had learned earlier in the year and all the pride they had came out in that game. Princeton stomped Providence 109–69, as Bradley scored 41 points.

"I had been a dominant factor in other games," Bradley told McPhee. "But in the Providence game I was a member of the greatest team I have ever played on."

The surprising Tigers were in the Final Four, the national semifinals, just one step away from playing for a national title. No Ivy League team had ever gone that far before, and certainly not the Princeton Tigers.

But the dream—for the team, at least—ended in the next game. Against a strong Michigan team, the same team they had almost beaten in December, Princeton struggled early and never caught up. Michigan won with a final score of 93–76.

In those days, however, the losers of the semifinals played another game for third place. Bill Bradley would lead the Princeton Tigers

36

against Wichita State University in his final college game. It would be one for the ages.

Not long after the game began, it was obvious that Princeton would win. Wichita was not up for the match, and Princeton's passing was superb. Bradley was scoring at will, but, of course, spent more time passing than shooting. With nine minutes remaining, the score was 84–58.

But, rather than take Bradley out, van Breda Kolff left him in. Soon, according to the *PAW* article, players on Princeton's bench and fans in the stands started urging Bradley to shoot more, to break the record of most points scored in an NCAA Tournament game.

Won over by the crowd's urgency, Bradley simply shot the ball for himself. After a career spent helping others succeed, he shot the lights out of the place . . . for himself.

He scored 26 points in those final nine minutes, including 16 points in the final five. In that time, he missed only one shot. He made hooks, layups, jump shots, and even a few circus shots. McPhee describes at length each of the shots, "arcing in, swishing in, the point total climbing and climbing."

Finally, Bradley reached 58 points, a new single-game record (he already had smashed the all-tournament record and helped Princeton set scoring records for the game and the tournament). With thirty-three seconds left, van Breda Kolff took Bradley out to an enormous standing ovation.

It was one of the most startling and memorable performances in college basketball history. The game, and the record, highlighted Bradley's career, but he didn't go home to celebrate.

Rather, according to the *PAW* article, he locked himself in a rented house for a month to finish his senior thesis. For Bill Bradley, it was always back to the books. Soon, though, it would be back to England.

# Going Pro

**B**ill Bradley's dreams of success in college—in the classroom and on the court—had come true. He had not only set new standards for excellence as a basketball player, he had met his own high standards for academics. He graduated with honors from Princeton and was named most likely to succeed and most popular.

His basketball skills also made him popular among pro scouts. In those days, NBA teams got first rights to college players in their geographic region. With their first pick in the 1965 NBA draft of college players, the New York Knicks chose Bradley.

Like everyone else, however, the Knicks knew that Bradley had other plans. The Oxford

dream that had first sent Bradley to Princeton had come true, too, and he headed to Europe in 1965.

While he thought he had put basketball behind him, his love for the game was still strong. Joining a group of top recent college graduates, he toured with the U.S. team in the World University Games, helping them win the gold medal.

# Finally a Rhodes Scholar

Bradley's long journey from Crystal City to England continued, and he settled in as a student at Worcester College, Oxford, to study philosophy, economics, and history. Not many great athletes ever turn down the chance to join the pros, but Bradley had different priorities. His restless mind outweighed his talented body. As great as he was at basketball, for him the game was always a means to an end, not an end in itself.

Though he was in a country where basketball was hardly played, he found a way to stay involved in the sport he loved. He eventually played for a team in Milan, Italy, traveling once or twice a month. The team competed all over Europe, so

Instead of jumping into professional basketball after Princeton, Bradley chose to study philosophy, economics, and history at Oxford.

Bradley got a chance to continue to fulfill his love for traveling. He struggled at times during the games, but he and the team bounced back winning the European Cup and defeating the team from the Soviet Union that Bradley and the U.S. team had beaten in the Olympics.

His studies in England revolved around reading, lectures, and discussions. Oxford has a history dating back more than 600 years as an international center of learning. The old stone buildings almost whisper a love of knowledge. Bradley reveled in the atmosphere, a place where he was simply another student, not a famous basketball player.

Even at the age of twenty-two, he had developed a deep sense of privacy. As an athlete, he had lived much of his life in the public eye. But he was then, and has remained, very uncomfortable with people prying into his personal life. It isn't surprising that living anonymously suited him well.

He did, however, participate in a variety of activities centered on his Christian faith. He met with local groups to talk about God, and he spoke at churches and schools. In one instance, he spoke at a large gathering organized by the famous American evangelist Billy Graham. But for the first time in his life, he was having doubts about his faith. He was uncomfortable with the narrow viewpoints of some Christians and of their occasional intolerance.

"Slowly, I began to see that Fundamentalism had a downside," he writes in *Time Present, Time Past*. "It did not tolerate debate, it did not seek balance. It appeared to be less a God-centered existence than a man-centered set of demands."

His discomfort reached its climax during a service at a church in Oxford. "The minister preached a sermon that blatantly defended white power in Rhodesia [an African nation, now called Zimbabwe, in which white people ruled a minority black population in a racist and often cruel way]. I walked out, never to return."

Questions about his faith and how it affected his views of the world continued to worry Bradley throughout his life.

Meanwhile, he continued his European travels. The summer after his first year at Oxford, he lived in Germany with a family for six weeks. He later spent his Christmas break in Bethlehem and Jerusalem. During these and other trips, he continued to spend time meeting people who lived in foreign lands, trying to understand their lives and situations. For Bradley, the fascination with life in other places that had started in his attic with *National Geographic* magazines was now a reality.

In *Time Present, Time Past*, he tells a story about his visit to Syria, where he waved to a young woman who lived next door. "I was warned by a representative of the hotel that under Islamic law the girl's father could have had my hand chopped off. I stopped waving."

He also traveled to the Soviet Union, exploring the capital city of Moscow and several other regions in that large nation. In those days, the Communist Party, an insular and paranoid government that was wary of foreigners, controlled that country. Bradley writes that his car was followed throughout his stay there.

"When we tried to leave the country and to cross into Hungary, we were detained by guards who searched our car and looked at every scrap of paper in our wallets," he writes in *Time Present, Time Past*. Bradley was carrying a small map that showed directions to a restaurant in Warsaw, Poland, but Soviet security claimed it was a spy map. He and his friends were eventually released, but the experience gave him great insight. While he continued to revel in his travels and his studies, Bradley knew that his time at Oxford was coming to an end. He wondered what to do next.

# Living His Dream

"Toward the end of my second year at Oxford, after not touching a basketball for nine months, I went into the Oxford gym for some long overdue exercise," he writes in *Life on the Run*, the famous book he wrote in 1975 about his experiences with the New York Knicks. "There I

shot alone—just the ball, the basket, and my imagination. I heard the swish and felt my body loosen into familiar movements—the jumper, the hook, the reverse pivot. I realized that I missed the game."

Already a draft pick of the Knicks, Bradley decided to join the team and turn pro. But he had one more mission to complete before beginning his professional career.

At that time, the summer of 1967, America was involved in the Vietnam War. Thousands of young men from the United States were serving in a conflict that many people back home in America thought was a bad idea. Bradley was not sure what he thought about the war at the time. He defended America when debating fellow students from other countries who objected to the fighting. But he defended America the nation, not necessarily its role in Vietnam. "By 1968, the error of our involvement [in Vietnam] had become evident to me," he writes in *Time Present, Time Past*. But he had not reached that conclusion by the time his


Bill Bradley is pictured here during his stint in the Air Force Reserve, where he served for six months in 1967.

Oxford years ended and, in fact, wrote that he considered joining the army with an eye to becoming a teacher at West Point.

Still, rather than be drafted and possibly sent to Vietnam, he joined the Air Force Reserve. He served six months at a base in San Antonio, Texas, in 1967. For several years after that, as required by the reserves, he served one weekend a month and two weeks every summer.

## New York, New York

Finally, his service completed, the former Missouri high school star reached the big time: New York City and the NBA. Bradley joined the Knicks in December 1967. He signed a contract that was one of the richest for a rookie in NBA history: $500,000 for his first four years as a pro. The big contract helped him earn the nickname "Dollar Bill," a name he never liked.

"My father always reminded me that basketball was a game," he writes. "When I first told him I was going to play professional

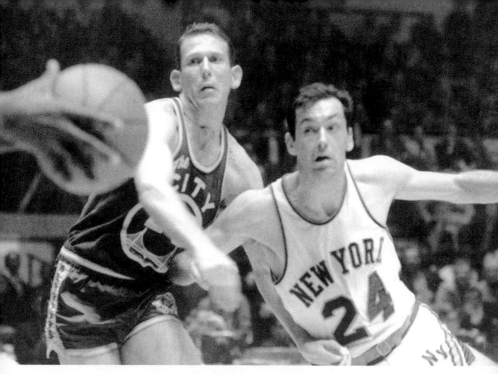

During a game in February 1968, Bradley, a rookie on the New York Knicks, tangles with the San Francisco Warriors' Jeff Mullins.

basketball, he asked 'When are you going to get a real job?' Then I told him what I'd be making. He replied, 'Not a bad job.'"

While basketball success had come quickly to Bradley in high school and college, his first days in the NBA were rocky ones. He didn't even start for the Knicks, and he was assigned to play guard when his natural position was as a forward. Ironically, his main competition for playing time was Cazzie Russell, the man who had helped Michigan defeat Bradley's Princeton team in the 1965 NCAA semifinals.

"I think that I'd lost the feel of the game," he once told the *Los Angeles Times*. "I wasn't into the flow of the game."

But true to his nature, Bradley learned his lessons. Though he played in only forty-five games as a rookie, he tried to learn all he could about life in the pros.

"For instance, when I came into the league, I took losses very hard," Bradley told NBA.com. "Once, when we had a tight game in Philadelphia, I made a bad pass that cost us the game. Dave DeBusschere [a veteran forward] came into the locker room and told me, 'You can't live like that. You have to get ready for the next game.' I learned from Dave that you can't make the bad past affect a positive future."

Though the team's fans probably didn't know it at the time, the addition of Bradley to an already solid team would create a very positive future for the Knicks.

# The Championship Season

**F**ollowing Bradley's first season with the Knicks, he took care of some unfinished business in England. At Oxford, he had postponed his final exams so he could begin his NBA career. Now, with a summer off from the game, he returned to school to cram for the big tests.

As he had after his incredible NCAA Tournament record-setting game, he turned to solitude for success. Rather than return to the dorms at Oxford, he stayed in a small motel near the city. For twelve hours a day, seven days a week, for more than three weeks, he studied, reviewed, and refreshed all the information he had taken in during his two-year course of study.

## Bill Bradley

# A Nation in Turmoil

As it would be throughout his life after college, a strong reality intervened into Bradley's smaller worlds of study and sports. About a week before exams, Bradley joined the world in being stunned by the assassination of Robert Kennedy. Just months earlier, Bradley had turned to the soothing and inspirational words of Kennedy when Dr. Martin Luther King Jr. had been assassinated.

The death of King had hit Bradley hard and renewed his interest and passion in civil rights; he would make it one of the central focuses of his personal and political career. But the double blow of Kennedy's death helped reinforce the vital need for public service. To Bradley, Kennedy was an example of life lived for others, of a person using his skills to help people.

In *Time Present, Time Past*, Bradley remembers a speech given by Senator Kennedy during the summer of 1964. In his speech to the young interns working for various government

52

Pallbearers carry Robert F. Kennedy's casket to its final resting place in Arlington National Cemetery in June 1968. Kennedy's life had a profound effect on Bradley's outlook and political philosophy.

offices, he said, "Public service is a noble profession, and politics a crucial skill." He urged Americans to accept less comfort themselves in order to give more people a better chance. He asked them to excel at being human.

Bradley also wrote, "Robert Kennedy seemed to have a deeper level of conviction, a fuller capacity for love, a keener perception of evil, and a more complete understanding of the fragility of life than most political candidates."

He was obviously deeply touched by Kennedy's wisdom and love of public service.

Bradley watched the funeral and the ceremonies honoring Kennedy from his lonely hotel room 3,000 miles from home. He would always carry the memories of his reaction with him. And so, Bradley's life pushed more firmly now in the direction that it would eventually follow resolutely.

Bradley passed his exams and earned degrees in politics, philosophy, and economics.

He was immediately able to use his skills to benefit others. Instead of enjoying time off before reporting back to the Knicks for preseason practice, Bradley took a job that was far away from his suburban upbringing. He spent the summer working in Harlem at the Urban League's Street Academy.

He taught reading to young students, wrote fund-raising letters and brochures, and worked with people to develop black-owned businesses. Through it all, he experienced life in what was then unflatteringly called the ghetto. While these programs were run by several Christian evangelists, many of the people Bradley worked with were part of the growing Black Muslim movement.

In an interview with *Esquire* magazine in February 2000, he remembered those months in Harlem. "What I didn't know until that summer was the urban subculture," he said. "I didn't know about everybody out on the street at night—families, aunts, and grandparents. That was the energy there. I didn't know the rhythms of the street."

It was just another instance of Bradley being open to new experiences and of how he let those new experiences help shape his thinking.

## The New York Knicks

Bradley returned to the Knicks for the 1968–1969 season, hoping to improve his play. He had spent some summer evenings playing in Philadelphia in the Baker League, made up of high-quality summer teams. As a pro, Bradley had been moved from forward to guard; in Philadelphia, he honed the skills he would need to continue that transition. He gained confidence playing in the rough-and-tumble league and returned to the Knicks ready to meet the challenges of the NBA.

Though he remained a guard, he began to see his play recover. Playing in every game, he improved his scoring average to 12.4 points per game. The lessons learned on the summer courts of Philadelphia paid off on the courts of the NBA.

On January 21, 1969, another player's misfortune became the turning point in Bradley's NBA career. Cazzie Russell, who had been Bradley's collegiate rival at Michigan and was now his teammate in New York, broke his ankle in a game at Madison Square Garden against the Seattle Supersonics.

Knicks coach Red Holzman was forced to alter his lineup to compensate for the loss of one of his star forwards. He switched Bradley from the position of guard to forward. The team, and Bradley, never looked back. Moved to his more natural position as forward and

New York Knicks coach Red Holzman watches his team take on the Boston
Celtics in the NBA playoffs on April 18, 1969.

freed from defending the often smaller and
quicker guards, Bradley flourished and the
team followed. From his wing positions, he was
able to use his tremendous passing skills to the
team's advantage.

"During a game," he writes in *Values of
the Game*, "what I loved most was spotting an
imbalance in the opponent's defense and
getting the ball to the open man at the right
time, and in the right place."

Bradley and the Knicks found themselves in just the right place at that time in NBA history. For the 1969–1970 season, they added power forward Dave DeBusschere to form one of the NBA's legendary starting fives: Bradley, DeBusschere, center Willis Reed, and guards Dick Barnett and Walt "Clyde" Frazier. Reed was the team leader, the captain, and the center of the offense, but he was more a part of their success than the single cause. Rather than starring individually, together they were nearly unstoppable.

Early in the season, New York won eighteen games in a row. With Bradley increasing his scoring to 14.5 points per game, Reed dominating the boards, and Frazier running the offense as point guard, the Knicks created the NBA's best record at 60–22. The team became hugely popular in New York, and their unselfish style of play was a change from most other star-dominated NBA teams.

In the first round of the playoffs, the Knicks needed seven games to defeat the Baltimore

Bullets. In the Eastern finals, they easily knocked off the Milwaukee Bucks in five games, setting the stage for one of the most dramatic NBA Finals series in history.

The Los Angeles Lakers had won the Western Division with twelve fewer wins than the Knicks, and thus the Knicks would have the home-court advantage. (That is, four of the seven games in the finals were scheduled for Madison Square Garden, including the seventh, if it was needed.)

While the Knicks were a team of players who filled their roles and meshed as a unit, the Los Angeles Lakers were anchored by three legendary stars: guard Jerry West, forward Elgin Baylor, and center Wilt Chamberlain. All three would eventually enter the Basketball Hall of Fame and were among the best ever at their positions.

Chamberlain was slowed by injuries for the Finals, but he was still one of the most dominant big men in basketball history. But in Game 1, Reed scored 37 points, and the Knicks

won in front of the Garden faithful, 124–112. The Lakers tied the series with a 105–103 win in New York.

In Los Angeles, the Lakers tied Game 3 on one of the most famous shots in NBA history. Trailing by two, West brought the ball upcourt after a rebound and heaved the ball from behind half-court toward his basket. The buzzer sounded as the ball was in the air. It swished through to tie the game as the Lakers' fans went wild. But New York overcame that stunning shot and won in overtime 111–108.

Once again, the Lakers tied the series in overtime with a win of their own. Then, early in Game 5, Reed suffered a torn leg muscle. He endured the painful injury for the rest of the game, while Bradley and his teammates helped guard the imposing Chamberlain. The Knicks hung on to win 107–100.

Bradley goes for a layup to score against the Baltimore Bullets at Madison Square Garden in 1969.

"After his injury, we went in the locker room [at halftime] and redesigned our whole offense," Bradley remembered in an interview on NBA.com. "We ran a zone offense against the Lakers, even though they were playing man-to-man [defense]. And we won that game."

But the team and its fans thought that their captain wouldn't be able to play for the rest of the series.

In Game 6, Chamberlain took advantage of Reed's absence and scored 45 points. The series was tied at three games apiece. On May 8, 1970, more than 18,000 fans crammed into the Garden to see the team that would have to take the floor minus Reed.

Bradley describes the scene in *Values of the Game*: "During warm-ups, West, Baylor, and Chamberlain limbered up for what they thought would be their first championship. Then Willis appeared from underneath the stands. The audience erupted in a roar like Niagara Falls."

Reed, knowing the importance of the moment, had done what his doctors said would be impossible: He prepared to play for the NBA title. The sight of him limping onto the court amid the din of the roaring crowd remains one of the most dramatic moments in sports history.

"And then the first time he touched the ball, he hit about an 18-footer and the crowd just went wild again," Bradley writes. "The first two minutes of the game sealed the Lakers' fate. They seemed dazed. The pressure had reached my childhood heroes."

Reed played only a few more minutes, scoring only 4 points. But inspired by his bravery and sense of the moment, Bradley and the Knicks roared to a convincing 113–99 victory, earning the team its first NBA championship and creating for Bradley a moment he would cherish forever.

"Everything I had gone through in my life seemed worth it for that one moment at center court on May 8, 1970," he writes in *Life on the Run*. "The championship vindicated my concept of, and approach to, the game [of basketball]. I had finally proved something to myself."

Bill Bradley, dedicated to practice, forged by his own will, honed by play among the best of the game, was now a champion.

# Life on the Run

Before the 1970–1971 NBA season, Bradley received news that would shape the rest of his basketball career. After three seasons competing with Cazzie Russell for playing time and the forward position, Bradley suddenly had the job all to himself. Knicks coach and general manager, Red Holzman, traded Russell to the San Francisco Warriors for Jerry Lucas.

"Red had picked me," Bradley writes in *Life on the Run*. "The effect was exhilarating. Before, when he had consulted me about strategy as he had with other players, I resented it, fearing it was some plot to cut my playing time. When Red came into the locker room and made some comment about Princeton . . . I burned with anger. But once Russell was gone,

A wide-eyed Bradley hustles the ball down the court during a game against the Seattle Supersonics.

things changed. I began to laugh when he kidded me about Princeton. The atmosphere became much more [friendly]."

However, Bradley and the rest of the Knicks could not repeat their success. Though they were the champions, the Knicks started the next season the same as the rest of the NBA. With Reed nursing injuries through most of the games, the Knicks made the playoffs, but they lost early.

Lucas had become a big part of the team by the 1971–1972 season, often subbing in for Reed at center. The team had also added flashy guard Earl "the Pearl" Monroe to join Walt Frazier in the backcourt. Bradley remained the sharp-shooting, eagle-eyed, passing forward, while DeBusschere handled the inside rebounding chores from the other forward position.

New York reached the NBA Finals again after that season, where once again they faced the Lakers and Chamberlain. Whereas in 1970, the Knicks had come in as favorites, this time around the Lakers were favored to win. Earlier in the season, Los Angeles had set an all-time record by winning thirty-three consecutive games. They had ended up with a league record of sixty-nine wins. To make matters worse, Reed would be unavailable for the Finals with another leg injury.

In Game 1, Bradley was unstoppable, hitting eleven of twelve shots in New York's surprising 114–92 victory in Los Angeles. But that would be the Knicks' last hurrah.

Chamberlain dominated the next four games, including scoring 29 points and grabbing 24 rebounds in the title-clinching Game 5. Bradley and the Knicks were 1–1 in NBA Finals. They soon had a chance to improve that record.

In the 1972–1973 season, New York was still a strong team. Bradley had his best pro season ever, setting career highs with an average of 16.1 points and 4.5 assists per game. He also continued a trend that he had begun during his second season in the league: outstanding free-throw shooting.

When a player is fouled, often the result is a shot called a free throw taken from eighteen feet directly in front of the basket with no one guarding the player. It looks easy, but NBA players must do it under the pressure of a packed arena. They have been running, jumping, and sweating, and then suddenly they have to stop, pause, and carefully aim a shot. Some players cannot master this skill. Bradley, however, among the league's top scoring players, had the concentration to make 84 percent of attempted free throws.

The Knicks did not win the Atlantic Division in 1973; the Boston Celtics did, winning only one less game than the Lakers' record total of 68. After beating Baltimore in the first round, the Knicks faced the Celtics for the Eastern title.

## Eastern Head to Head

The battle between the two teams was always a tough one. The cities themselves were seen as rivals, both old, northeastern urban centers. In baseball, the New York Yankees and Boston Red Sox waged a dozen hard-fought battles each season. In hockey, the New York Rangers and Boston Bruins were old foes. The Celtics had dominated basketball in the 1960s, but now the Knicks were a worthy opponent, and their rivalry joined the older, more established Boston–New York grudge matches.

But with the tag-team duo of Reed and Lucas at center, and the still-strong quartet of Frazier, Monroe, Bradley, and DeBusschere playing in high gear, the underdog Knicks defeated mighty Boston in seven games.

In *Life on the Run*, Bradley remembers Holzman's reaction. "He stood in the locker room throwing right hands of jubilation at imaginary opponents. 'It's days like this that do it,' Red said to me. 'You get hooked, this job, this profession, you live for days like this.'"

These fruitful days would go on for the Knicks. Facing the Lakers in the NBA Finals for the third time in four seasons, the Knicks avenged their loss of the season before. After losing Game 1, they swept the Lakers in the next four, earning their second NBA title in four years. In the final game, five Knicks players scored in double figures.

In *Life on the Run*, Bradley remembers that this second title was quieter. "It was a more mature victory, [subtly] savored instead of excitedly consumed. The euphoria lasted during the post-game meal with friends, through a marvelous night, and through the plane ride back to New York. But by the following day, it was over."

The intensely private Bradley, pictured here with his wife, Ernestine Schlant, has been careful to separate his public and private lives.

# Wedding Vows

Though he dated throughout his NBA career, Bradley was never serious about anyone until he met Ernestine Schlant, a former German national living in New York and teaching German literature. She lived in Bradley's apartment building with her daughter from a previous marriage. In her, he found an intellectual equal; she didn't even know that he played basketball when they first met.

He loved her for many reasons, but partly because she loved him as just Bill, not as Bill Bradley, the basketball star. He also loved that she was as smart as he was (and in some ways more so), speaking five languages and having a wide knowledge of literature.

She and Bradley were married in 1974; they had a daughter, Theresa, in 1976. Ernestine did eventually learn to love basketball, although she would sometimes be seen in the stands at Knicks games reading a book instead of watching her husband play. Apparently, he didn't mind at all.

# A Political Future for an NBA Star

Bradley was a rare athlete who was able to give himself fully to a sport and, at the same time, maintain an ability to look at it from a distance. His book *Life on the Run*, written during the 1974–1975 season, is a compelling sports biography, giving a moving look into life as a professional athlete in the actual words of a player, not a sportswriter.

Boston Celtic John Havlicek makes a futile attempt to block a shot by Bill Bradley during the NBA Eastern Conference Finals in April 1974.

One of the book's greatest strengths is Bradley's intimate story of his teammates. Reading it, you realize, as he did, that these are more than men in uniform, more than collections of statistics and baskets. Each player that Bradley played with is shown as a person; as a man. He learned many things from his teammates: the power of the mind from Lucas, the power of friendship from DeBusschere, the experience of life as a black man in America from Reed and Monroe, and discipline from Frazier. Bradley also describes life on the road, the endless chain of hotels, airplanes, arenas, buses, and trains, that NBA players experience during a typical season.

"From the middle of September until May, there is usually no longer than one day at a time without basketball," he writes. "There are no long weekends or holidays for players."

The lifestyle was encompassing, but even during his relentless traveling, Bradley was always moving toward his post-NBA career.

He played as hard as he could, but for him, the NBA was a pathway to the future.

"Being on a championship team is like [floating on a raft down the Mississippi, like Huck Finn]. Neither one can last forever," Bradley writes.

During his final four years in the NBA, Bradley spent a great deal of time during and between seasons working toward his future. As he went around the league, he visited politicians in each city, asking more about what they did and how they ran their campaigns.

"I just went around—does this sound funny?—looking for America," he told the *New York Times Magazine* in 1978.

A Democrat, he learned about the issues that his party thought were important. He helped fight for civil rights, and he learned about environmental issues and how to reform welfare. One summer, he worked in Washington, D.C., at the Office for Economic Development, which helped small businesses and minorities improve their lives and work.

As early as 1970, teammates were teasing him about his Princeton education, asking whether he'd be president someday. His interest in politics and public policy made a political career seem like a certain possibility.

"Yes, basketball was a means to an end [in politics]," he said in the *New York Times Magazine* article. "It gave me the time and opportunity to prepare for politics. I chose it from the outset with that kind of jump in mind when it was over."

Still, Bradley worried about his future. "What is left after basketball," he writes about life beyond the court, "is to live all one's days never able to recapture the feeling of those few years of intensified youth . . . I have often wondered how I will handle the end of my playing days. No one really knows until the day comes."

For Bill Bradley, that day came after the 1977 season.

# New Challenges

"The abruptness of the season's end strikes me. For eight months, you play basketball and think about basketball; your happiness depends on basketball. Then it is over. Nothing fills the void."

Bradley, however, had found something to fill the void. It was finally the right time to enter the political life toward which he had been aiming since his experiences in Washington, D.C. He announced that he would run for the United States Senate, representing the state of New Jersey.

Bradley was taking on another contest, and it would take more than a sweet jump shot to make him a winner in this game.

# Senator Bradley

**R**ather than try for election to a lesser office back home, or to a lower-profile seat in his native Missouri, Bradley decided to run for the United States Senate of New Jersey, which had become his home during his NBA career.

He was not, however, supported by the Democratic Party in New Jersey, which backed another candidate. But Bradley's enormous popularity overcame the objections of career politicians.

"I ran as a citizen-politician," he writes in *Time Present, Time Past.* "I played up the fact that I had taken a different road to a Senate candidacy from my opponents in the primary. Although I had no experience in government, I had appeared in people's living rooms for ten years. They had seen me perform as a player; they felt they knew me."

And for those who *didn't* know him, Bradley paid close attention. Throughout the spring leading up to the primary, he traveled the length of New Jersey, spending eighteen-hour days meeting people and talking about his vision for the state.

"In one memorable day," he wrote in *Time Present, Time Past*, "I campaigned in all of the state's twenty-one counties, starting at a diner at 4:30 AM and ending at another diner at 10 PM."

## A Classic Democrat

Bradley carefully outlined his views. He called for increased rights for women and stronger sentences for convicted felons, although he was against capital punishment (the death penalty). In foreign affairs, he called for talks in the Middle East. He felt that President Jimmy Carter's proposed 20 percent tax cut was too high. He also began talking about alternative sources of energy because of a recent gasoline shortage.

"We've got to develop new industries in solar energy, in pollution control, to make things that people here and abroad are going to need," Bradley told the *New York Times Magazine*.

But his greatest call was for equality, especially as it related to race. His experiences in the NBA and in the Harlem summer school opened his eyes to America's continual racial problems. Working toward greater racial equality would be a constant theme of Bradley's public life.

Bradley wrote about the racial lessons he had learned with the Knicks in his book *Values of the Game*. "You can't play on a team with African Americans for very long and fail to recognize the stupidity of our national obsession with race. The right path is really very simple. Give respect to teammates of a different race, treat them fairly, disagree with them honestly, enjoy their friendship, explore your common humanity, share your thoughts candidly, work for a common goal and help each other achieve it."

Bradley felt strongly throughout his life in politics that this lesson learned on the court should be applied to life.

Bradley's famous face and hard work helped him win the Democratic primary, winning more than 60 percent of the votes. In the general election in November, he faced Republican candidate Jeffrey Bell, another young man fairly green to politics. Bell's key plan was a call for a 30 percent cut in income taxes.

Bradley and Bell debated more than twenty times before the November vote. Bradley called on his experiences as a player once again to help him prepare and succeed in the debates. During his NBA years, he had made many speeches to a wide variety of groups. This experience in public speaking helped him look confident in the political debates.

His NBA connections helped in other ways; many players contributed money or time to his campaign, as did many former Princeton classmates.

Newly sworn in as a senator, Bill Bradley shares a joke with Vice President Walter Mondale, family, and friends in January 1979.

In the end, it worked. The young man from Missouri had gone from basketball hero to U.S. senator. Bradley defeated Bell with 56 percent of the vote. In January 1979, when he was sworn in, Bradley became the youngest man in the Senate. He was thirty-five years of age.

## Celebrity Status

Although Bradley had spent most of his adult life on the public stage, he was never comfortable talking about himself or having others ask about his private life. As he became more important and well known, first as an NBA player and then as a politician, this became a bigger problem. People—mostly reporters—wanted to know more about his private life, but Bradley fought harder to keep it separate from his public, political life.

John Phillips, author of a lengthy *New York Times Magazine* article that appeared just before Bradley's election to the Senate, commented at length about how Bradley seemed to be both asking for people's attention and hiding from it at the same time.

"Look, I know what they've always said," Bradley replied. "I'm stuffy or whatever. But politics is what I've always wanted, what I've pointed for all along. It's a much bigger part of my existence. The public [attention] doesn't consume me. Sure, they wear me out. It's part of the price you pay. I still have a core of privacy. Everybody does, and ought to. But it's smaller now, so I cherish it."

# The Political Grind

With the election won, Bradley now moved into life as a senator. He worked hard to learn the rules of the Senate and all he could about the issues. For most of his first year, he was fairly quiet, spending much of his time reading and meeting with people. He was also proving that he belonged, that he could do the work, and that he hadn't been elected simply for his basketball fame.

Like all senators, he was assigned to various committees that work with legislation. This included the Energy and Natural Resources Committee, which dealt with energy policy, water and power, and mineral resources, and the Finance Committee, which worked on tax matters.

From all of these committees, he helped guide bills into law. As an acknowledged expert in energy, he helped add more to the nation's petroleum reserves. In the health care field, he sponsored a bill that helped the aged and disabled stay at home more easily, rather than be forced into nursing homes. In foreign affairs, he called on his experiences in Europe when he

During his first term as a United States senator, Bradley was inducted into the Basketball Hall of Fame in Springfield, Massachusetts.

returned to Russia to meet with Soviet leaders about a missile treaty.

Like a good politician, he didn't forget families, helping to save thousands of jobs for New Jersey residents and finding funds to save the pristine New Jersey Pinelands National Reserve.

Four years into his first term in the Senate, Bradley was elected to the Basketball Hall of Fame in Springfield, Massachusetts. He was joined by his old teammate Dave DeBusschere. While it is generally regarded as the ultimate accomplishment for a player—and Bradley was indeed honored—he looked on his basketball life as part of his past.

## Bradley's Famous Beach Walks

Almost before Bradley knew it, it was time to run again. For his second campaign, in 1986, he developed what would become a signature of his tenure in the Senate: the beach walk.

As part of his continuing work to meet with the citizens of his state, he had developed what he called "walking town meetings." He would go to a town or a mall and just walk around, meeting people, listening to their comments, and answering their questions. Since New Jersey has a long coastline, he made beach walks part of this strategy. He would stride the sand, right on the water's edge, preceded by aides carrying signs that read "Meet Senator Bill Bradley." The walks, and his work in Washington, helped, and he won reelection.

Senator Bradley enjoys a light-hearted moment on a beach during one of his weekly "walking town meetings," in New Jersey.

Among his first tasks was to continue work to support the massive 1986 Tax Reform Act. The bill, which he had championed and which had passed at the end of his first term, created many important changes in the nation's tax laws. Many were originally Bradley's ideas, but some came from and were supported by Republican president Ronald Reagan. Bradley's support of a Reagan plan angered many Democrats, but he stuck to his guns.

"Tax reform, in defiance of the odds, upheld the public interest against the special interest," he writes in *Time Present, Time Past*. "The bill was based on equity, simplicity, and efficiency." It became one of Bradley's biggest successes in the Senate.

# From Tax Reform to the CIA

Another area in which he became more involved was intelligence, or, in other words, the operations of our government that find out things about other governments. The Senate Committee on Intelligence oversees the budget of the Central Intelligence Agency (CIA) and other parts of government charged with what is essentially spying.

Bradley learned the ins and outs of how spies work and how the budgets, priorities, and operations of intelligence have real-life consequences. In one particular area of the world, once again his previous travels came into play. In the 1980s, the Soviet Union had invaded the country of Afghanistan. Bradley supported helping rebels fighting the Soviets, partly because of his visits there during an off season from the Knicks. Friends he made among the Afghani Kush people assisted him in working to help the rebels.

As the Cold War ended in the 1990s, Bradley worked within the intelligence community to help organize what it would do next. Throughout, his goal was similar to what he worked for in domestic politics: understanding and unity through study and knowledge.

"A key to our world leadership as a democracy with a growing economy is our understanding of other cultures," he writes in *Time Present, Time Past.* "What is essential is that we now look outward and avoid being consumed by inward-looking, shortsighted politics."

In 1990, Bradley had a close call in his next reelection campaign. Expecting an easy win, he only narrowly defeated Christine Todd Whitman. Part of many people's reason for voting against their two-term senator was his refusal to criticize Governor Jim Florio for a series of tax hikes. Florio had been one of the first New Jersey politicians to back Bradley, and Bradley's loyalty almost cost him a job.

Many people say that the close call changed Bradley, making him less fond of politics and more cautious about his decisions. Whether that was the reason or not, it would be his last senatorial election.

## Family Values

In 1992, Bradley and his family went through a difficult crisis. Ernestine Schlant, Bradley's wife, was diagnosed with breast cancer. Throughout her struggle, Bradley remained with her, helping her through the treatments. When he could get away, he would spend many hours alone, reading books about cancer and its treatments and therapies.

She eventually recovered, but even after it was over, many people and staff who were close to Bradley knew nothing about it. Again it was an instance of him keeping his personal life private. Many politicians would have made a big deal of their support of their wives, but not Bradley. He did, however, credit the episode with making him more aware of speaking from his heart, of being emotional when it was appropriate.

Bradley continued working in the Senate, but he was once again aiming at another goal. In 1995, he announced that he would not seek a fourth term in the Senate. He said, "Politics is broken," and that he wanted to step away from it all to see where else his life would go.

Many people who had known Bill Bradley were not at all surprised at his next move.

# The Road Ahead

I have no second thoughts about leaving," Bradley told *Esquire* magazine in 2000 about his decision to leave the Senate. "I had a wonderful eighteen years. I represented my state and country the best I could, but it was time to move on. I made sure that a Democrat succeeded me, and then went on to a deeper encounter with the American people."

Bradley spent the first two and a half years after he left the Senate traveling, working, and teaching. He worked for a company on Wall Street, and he wrote *Time Present, Time Past*. He worked in television and made countless speeches.

Among his teaching posts were stops at the University of Notre Dame, the University of Maryland, and Stanford University. His former Princeton roommate Dan Okimoto introduced him to many important leaders of the "new economy" in Silicon Valley. Also while at Stanford, he once again became a fan of basketball, attending many university games and helping the players with new plays during practices. Through it all, the aim, first in the back of his mind, then in the front, was a run for the U.S. presidency.

Even as a young man in Crystal City and later as a player in the NBA, Bradley had been thought of as the type of person who would "one day be president." Bradley himself knew full well that a run for the presidency was his destiny. Even as early as 1987, he had laid down four ideas that he would have to deal with before he would consider running. These were firsthand knowledge of the country, a complete knowledge of foreign policy, a team of people to govern with, and excellent skills as a public speaker.

Bradley makes a basket in the backyard court of his childhood home in Crystal City, Missouri, just before kicking off his presidential campaign from his hometown in September 1999.

# Perchance to Dream

With President Bill Clinton ending his second and final term in 2000, and with Vice President Al Gore apparently vulnerable, Bradley knew that this was his chance. He had met every one of his four criteria by traveling extensively, becoming a foreign policy expert, attracting a group of other leaders, and constantly improving his communications skills.

Virtually every part of his life would come into play and be used to help convince America that Bill Bradley should be their president.

His storybook boyhood and his love for his parents would be the basis of speeches. His great education and intelligence, developed at Princeton and Oxford, would prove that he could handle the many aspects of the job. His eighteen years in the Senate would show that he was familiar with government and knew a great deal about both foreign and domestic policy. Bill Bradley had all the qualifications for the presidency. Now he just had to convince people outside New Jersey to vote for him. In September 1999, he officially announced his candidacy in his hometown of Crystal City, Missouri.

"I don't do anything that I don't want to win," he told *Rolling Stone* magazine a few weeks later. "I wouldn't have gotten into this if I couldn't see my way through to 270, which is the number of electoral votes needed to win. I'm putting everything I have into this race."

Bill Bradley gathers with several former teammates from the Knicks during a presidential campaign fund-raiser called "Back in the Garden" at Madison Square Garden in November 1999.

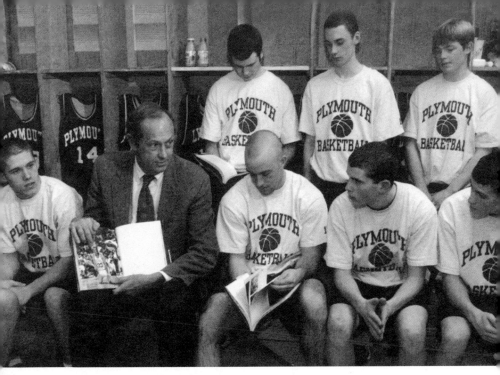

On a three-day campaign stop in New Hampshire, Bradley shows the Plymouth Regional High School varsity basketball team his favorite photograph from his book *Values of the Game.*

Bradley had some initial success, doing well in New Hampshire and Iowa, charming small-town people and big-city Democrats alike. The themes of his campaign were the same ones that he had spoken about as a U.S. senator: racial equality, spreading prosperity, and better health care for more people.

*Time* magazine wrote, "Bradley approaches campaigning the way he approached basketball:

by analysis and repetition, breaking down every shot down to its parts, then mastering them."

Yet the signs of his old struggles with privacy were showing. Reporters couldn't get him to talk about himself in the way that other politicians did. Bradley's laid-back manner of speaking and his reluctance to answer questions about himself began to make him look less than presidential. He wouldn't name his favorite books or even say where he went to church, "That's where I draw the line," he told *Time* magazine.

Bradley just could not shake his lifelong compulsion for privacy; many wondered why he ran at all, knowing that the campaign almost required complete disclosure of everything in your life.

"You do have to share a certain amount," he told *Time*. "I think I have. But you certainly don't have to share everything."

But that is, in fact, what people expected. Bradley might have been a brilliant senator, an intelligent and caring man, and a respected

leader, but many Americans just couldn't warm up to him. And most people blamed Bradley's worries about privacy for the public's "frozen" opinion of him.

Suddenly it seemed it was over. On Super Tuesday, March 13, 2000, when hundreds of electoral votes are decided, Bradley lost every one of the primaries to Vice President Gore. All the work, all the effort, seemingly a lifetime of working to this point, in the end were not enough. Whether it was just not the right time, or he was just not the right man, Bill Bradley conceded something he had not faced in many years: defeat.

"I once wrote that defeat has a richness of experience all its own," Bradley said. "That's probably true here, too."

The public life of a most private man was essentially over, not with the buzzer of a basketball game, but with the clicks of thousands of levers in voting booths.

Still, Bill Bradley remains a remarkable and unique American success story. He is a

Bradley waves a final good-bye to the media and his supporters as he drops out of the presidential race.

small-town boy who longed to see the world, a basketball star who wanted more out of life than just sports, and a man who achieved political greatness.

In October 2000, former U.S. senator Bill Bradley signs copies of his latest book, *The Journey From Here*, at a California bookstore.

# glossary

**alumnus**   Graduate of a school or university.

**amateur**   In sports, a person who is not paid to play sports, such as a college player or Olympic athlete; a nonprofessional athlete.

**arthritis**   Painful condition that is caused by inflammation of the joints.

**assist**   A pass from one player to another that leads directly to a basket.

**backboard**   The six-by-four foot board that is fixed behind the basket rim, usually made of wood or Plexiglas.

**basket**   The hoop through which the ball must go for a player to score; a field goal.

**center**   Usually the tallest player on a team's starting unit; the player most responsible for plays closest to the basket, including rebounding, scoring, and shot blocking.

**court**   The playing space for a basketball game, measuring ninety-four feet long; also called the floor.

**criteria**   Standards on which a judgment can be based.

**din**   Loud, confused, or prolonged noise.

**dunk**   Act of slamming the ball through the basket with one or both hands.

**economics**   Science of the production and distribution of goods and services.

**evangelist**   A person who preaches his or her religious faith and tries to convert others to it.

**forward**   One of the two players flanking the center, usually on offense.

**foul**   An illegal move or contact as witnessed by the referee.

**free throw**   An uncontested shot, worth one point, taken by a player who has been fouled. The number of shots depend of the situation of the foul. Also called a foul shot.

**fundamentalism**   A Protestant movement holding the Bible to be the sole historical and prophetic authority.

**guard**   One of two rear players on a team, usually shorter and quicker than the forwards and the center. Guards are responsible for advancing the ball up the court and shooting from long distance.

**NBA**   National Basketball Association, founded in 1949. The NBA currently has twenty-nine teams in the United States and Canada.

**pass**   To move the ball from one player to another, which may or may not include the ball making a single bounce on the court.

**rebound**   To retrieve the ball as it bounces off the rim or backboard, taking possession of it for either team.

**rookie**   Player in his or her first professional season.

**thesis**   Lengthy essay or other written article that one must complete to receive certain academic degrees.

The Naismith Memorial Basketball Hall of Fame
1150 West Columbus Avenue
Springfield, MA 01105
(413) 781-6500
(877) 4HOOPLA (446-6752)
Web sites: http://www.hoophall.com
http://www.basketballhalloffame.com
The Naismith Memorial Basketball Hall of Fame,
established in 1968, honors players who have made
a significant contribution to the sport. Each year, a
panel of experts elects a new group of individuals to
join those already honored.

## Web Sites

Bill Bradley's Web Site
http://www.billbradley.com
The National Basketball Association (NBA)
http://www.nba.com/history
Along with current statistics and results from NBA
teams and players, this site features a good history
section about past NBA greats.

# Bill Bradley

Princeton University
http://www.princeton.edu
The Web site for Princeton University contains
links to the athletic department, basketball team,
and *Princeton Alumni Weekly*, a newsletter that
can be searched for a large number of articles
relating to Bill Bradley.

*The Washington Post*
http://www.washingtonpost.com/onpolitics
The *Washington Post* Web site features coverage of
a wide number of people in politics, including
recent presidential candidates such as Bill Bradley.

## for further reading

Andryszewski, Tricia. *Bill Bradley: Scholar, Athlete, Statesman.* Brookfield, CT: Millbrook Press, 1999.

Bradley, Bill. *The Journey from Here.* New York: Artisan, 2000.

Bradley, Bill. *Life on the Run.* New York: Vintage Books, 1995.

Bradley, Bill. *Time Present, Time Past: A Memoir.* New York: Vintage Books, 1997.

Bradley, Bill. *Values of the Game.* New York: Artisan, 1998.

McPhee, John. *A Sense of Where You Are: A Profile of Bill Bradley at Princeton.* 2nd ed. New York: Noonday Press, 1995.

# index

# Index

# Author's Note

On a personal note, Bill Bradley has been a political hero of mine for many years. I was too young to really appreciate him as a player, so it was thrilling to learn about his outstanding basketball career in greater detail. I hope you have enjoyed reading about this complex and vastly talented person who allowed strong personal principles to guide him throughout his life, no matter the stakes. Thanks for reading.

—James Buckley Jr.
Santa Barbara, CA, 2001

# About the Author

James Buckley Jr. is a veteran sportswriter who has worked for *Sports Illustrated* and the National Football League. He is the author of more than twenty books for young people on a variety of sports. The editorial director of the Shoreline Publishing Group, he lives in Santa Barbara, California, with his wife and two children.

# Photo Credits

# Series Design and Layout

Geri Giordano